Your Career

Thinking About Jobs and Careers

J. Michael Farr and Susan Christophersen

Publisher: J. Michael Farr
Project Director: Spring Dawn Reader
Editor: Greg Croy
Production Editor: Sara Hall
Cover Design: Robert Pawlak
Illustration Selection and Arrangement: Mike Kreffel
Interior Design: Coventry Graphics/Spring Dawn Reader
Composition: Kay Mueller

Career & Life Skills Series: *Your Career-Thinking About Jobs and Careers*
©1991, **JIST Works, Inc.**, Indianapolis, IN

Send all inquiries to:
JIST Works, Inc.
720 North Park Avenue • Indianapolis, IN 46202-3431
Phone: (317) 264-3720 • FAX: (317) 264-3709

ISBN: 0-942784-60-X

About This Book

This book is about making choices. You make choices everyday—or put off making them—which is choosing too. Some choices are much more important than others. The important choices are what this book is about. You will learn about an easy-to-use process that you can use when you need to make important choices. We think you can't afford NOT to learn how to make good choices. Which is why we wrote this book. We know you will benefit from it.

Other Books in *The Career & Life Skills Series:*

This book is one of four books in the Career & Life Skills Series. The titles in the series include:

Knowing Yourself–Learning About Your Skills, Values and Planning Your Life: This book provides a specific process for clarifying your values and defining your unique skills. This new knowledge is then used as a basis for defining a successful lifestyle through a series of worksheets.

Making Decisions–Learning to Take Control of Your Life: This book presents a simple and memorable three step process for making good decisions. This three step process is then used to practice making meaningful short- and long-term life decisions through a series of worksheets.

Your Career–Thinking About Jobs and Careers: Factors that are often overlooked in career decision-making—such as values, skills, preferences for work environment and many others—are reviewed in this book. These decision-making tools are then used to identify careers for additional exploration through a series of worksheets. Major career information sources are also explored.

Career Preparation–Getting the Most from Training and Education: This book presents tips for getting the most out of your school experience. It stresses the increased earnings and other advantages for those finishing school. Additional training and educational options are presented and career planning/education worksheets provided for additional focus.

Instructors may obtain copies of these books from their dealer or from the publisher. Quantity discounts are available.

Table of Contents

Part II

Part III

Intro

Choosing the Right Career

How many times have you heard the question, "What do you want to be when you grow up?" When you were younger, the idea of growing up and striking out on your own was off in the distant future. What you might be when you "grew up" was just a fantasy.

Now, that future is becoming less distant all the time. You are growing up. The fantasies of childhood are behind you. The time is coming when you will start making real choices about your life as an adult.

You may still hold on to hopes and dreams from your younger years. (Some people really do grow up to be firefighters!) But whether you've had a lifelong dream or still aren't sure what you want to do, it's time to start taking

action. It's time to gather information so that when you're ready, you can decide what it is you want, figure out how to get it, and then start making it happen.

Fantasies are fun. But soon, you are going to be making choices that affect your lifestyle, your education, and your career goals. It's time to use your imagination to think about what you really want and how you can make that happen. This book can help you get started.

But be ready to do some legwork! Exploring career possibilities involves talking with people and using various resources to gather information. Learning to combine your imagination with solid skills and information is what this book is all about.

Part I

What Kind of Work Suits You?

Jobs and Careers

See if you can answer this question: What is the difference between a job and a career? Write your answer in the spaces below.

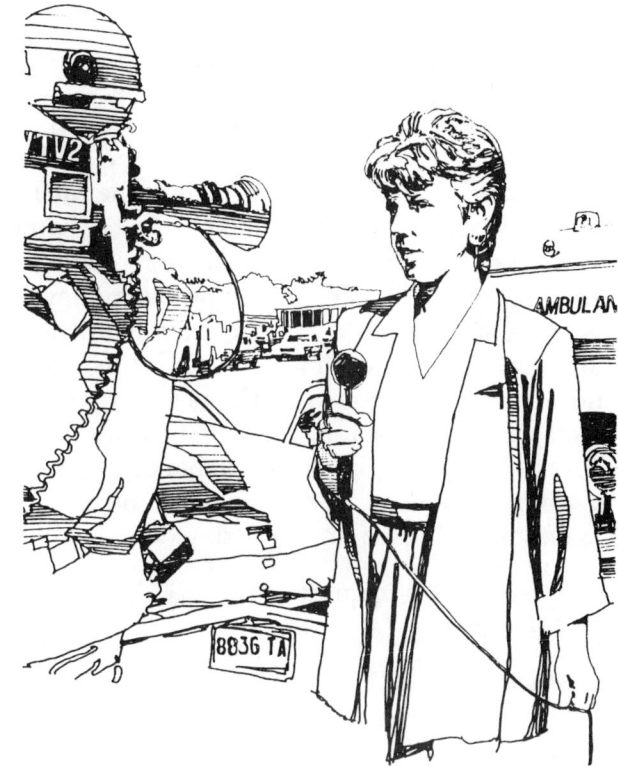

A job is:

_____

_____

_____

_____

_____

A career is:

_____

_____

_____

_____

A job is performing work and getting paid for it. It may be part of a career or it may not. Read the story about Pete and Carlos to see what this means.

Pete and Carlos's Story

Pete and Carlos work together at a fast food restaurant. They flip hamburgers on the grill, fry French fries, and perform many other tasks. They work the same shifts and collect the same pay. But each of them has a different reason for working at this job. Pete is saving his money to pay for classes and expenses related to vocational training in auto mechanics. Carlos, on the other hand, plans to work his way up to manager of the restaurant where he now works. Eventually, he hopes to manage even bigger restaurants and perhaps become an owner or partner of one someday.

Now answer these questions:

1. What is Pete's "job?"

_____

2. What is Pete's "career?"

_____

3. What is Carlos's "job?"

_____

4. What is Carlos's "career?"

_____

Pete and Carlos have the same job. But each is on a different career path. Pete is headed toward the field of auto mechanics, where he will eventually choose a particular job within that field. Pete's job helps provide the money he needs to get into the career he has chosen.

Carlos's job may help him pay for courses related to restaurant management, but it also puts him on his own career path. He is already working an entry level job in the restaurant field, which is what he has chosen for his career.

Why Do People Work?

Many people take a variety of jobs without having a career path in mind. You can make a living without having a career. But most people find that earning an income is only one of the reasons they work. There are other important reasons for working; let's explore some of those reasons.

A Survey of People Who Work and Their Reasons for Working

Talk to three adults who work. You can choose parents, teachers, family, friends, or anyone you want. Ask the questions found on the following worksheet summarizing their answers.

Worker Survey—Reasons for Working Worksheet

Person's Name: _____ Company Name: _____

1. Why do you work?

_____

_____

_____

2. If you didn't have to work for money, would you want to work anyway? Why?

_____

_____

_____

3. If you had the choice, would you keep this job or would you do something else?

_____

_____

_____

4. Make a list of the things you like and don't like about working.

   Things I like about working:

_____

_____

_____

   Things I don't like about working:

_____

_____

_____

Worker Survey—Reasons for Working Worksheet

Person's Name: _____ Company Name: _____

1. Why do you work?

   _____

   _____

   _____

2. If you didn't have to work for money, would you want to work anyway? Why?

   _____

   _____

   _____

3. If you had the choice, would you keep this job or would you do something else?

   _____

   _____

   _____

4. Make a list of the things you like and don't like about working.

   Things I like about working:

   _____

   _____

   _____

   Things I don't like about working:

   _____

   _____

   _____

Worker Survey—Reasons for Working Worksheet

Person's Name: _____ Company Name: _____

1. Why do you work?

   _____

   _____

   _____

2. If you didn't have to work for money, would you want to work anyway? Why?

   _____

   _____

   _____

3. If you had the choice, would you keep this job or would you do something else?

   _____

   _____

   _____

4. Make a list of the things you like and don't like about working.

   Things I like about working:

   _____

   _____

   _____

   Things I don't like about working:

   _____

   _____

   _____

What Did You Find Out?

Did you find out some reasons for working other than earning money? Look over your worksheets and make a list of those reasons below.

_____

_____

_____

_____

_____

Compare your list with the following one. These include the most common reasons people give for working:

Why People Work

- ■ To earn money for themselves or their family
- ■ To use their skills
- ■ To make a contribution to the community
- ■ To achieve status or prestige
- ■ To feel pride and a sense of accomplishment
- ■ To socialize with other people and have a way to meet people
- ■ To have a sense of belonging
- ■ To spend time doing something constructive

Values, Rewards, and Work

As you can see, there are lots of reasons to work. For many people, there is more to work than just earning a living. The exercise you just completed identified some of the values people find in their work to make it rewarding to them. If you don't know what you value, you are less likely to feel a sense of reward.

Read the story about Jack to see what this means.

Jack's Ideal Job

Jack was the envy of his friends. He seemed to have it all: a job with great benefits, a high income, and lots of prestige. Everybody in town seemed to know who he was.

But Jack wasn't happy, and it took him a while to figure out why. He finally realized that being the center of attention wasn't that important to him. What he really wanted, in fact, was a job with a lot less contact with people. He wanted work with less pressure and more time to work out ideas fully.

Jack realized that he was more of a "behind-the-scenes" kind of person. He was happier working with smaller groups of people in a quiet atmosphere. Jack's friends were surprised when he changed jobs. But after a while, they noticed that he seemed much happier.

What Rewards Do You Want?

Think about what rewards you hope to find in a job. Use the "Why People Work" list for ideas, and list any other rewards that come to mind.

_____

_____

_____

_____

_____

_____

_____

_____

_____

_____

Job Traits That Suit You

Do you like to be busy? Do you like to be in charge of things? Do you like to spend a lot of your time alone or with people? Do you like a noisy atmosphere or a quiet one? These are the kinds of things to think about when you are deciding what job "traits" match your personality and lifestyle.

It's hard to change your personality to fit the conditions found at a job. It's much better to choose work that fits YOU. For example, if constant noise around you is irritating, then working in a noisy office or on a demolition team probably won't make you happy.

Job Traits Checklist

A high noise level is an example of a job trait. Listed below are some others. Put a check next to the ones that appeal to you. Blanks in the far right column of this checklist are for traits you feel are important but were not listed.

Although you will make compromises on any job you take, you will be happier with a job that combines as many traits as possible you feel are important.

Job Traits Checklist

_____Work indoors

_____Work outdoors

_____A lot of responsibility

_____Not much responsibility

_____9 to 5 office work

_____Frequent traveling

_____Exciting, fast-paced

_____Slow, steady pace

_____Large organization

_____Small company

_____Work with your hands

_____Work with people

_____Use problem-solving ability

_____Usually confined (stay in one place — truck drivers, office workers for example)

_____Instruct others

_____Repetitious work

_____Dangerous work

_____Physical stamina required

_____Work requiring precision

_____Paying attention to detail

_____Frequent public contact

_____Part-time hours only

_____Creativity

_____Have influence over others

_____Work as part of a team

_____Work involving travel

_____

_____

_____

_____

_____

_____

_____

Identifying Your Skills

What Are You Good At?

Everyone is good at something. In fact, most people are good at many things and don't give themselves credit for them. You may take for granted many things you do well that others would find hard to do.

Knowing what you do best is important when you are deciding what kind of work is right for you. In your career, it makes sense to do the things you do best. If you do, you will probably be more successful.

It is also important to do things you enjoy doing. If you enjoy what you do and you're good at it, too, your life will be more satisfying.

Three Types of Skills

One way to define your skills is to organize them into three groups:

Job Content Skills: These are skills you need for a specific job. An auto mechanic, for example, needs to know how to tune up engines, repair brakes, and so on.

Adaptive Skills: These are often defined as personality or personal characteristics. They help a person adapt to or get along in a new situation. For example, honesty and enthusiasm are traits employers look for in a good worker.

Transferable Skills: These are skills you can use in many different jobs. You can transfer them from one job to another. Writing clearly and being well organized, for instance, are skills you can use in almost any job.

Knowing Your Skills Pays Off

It is important that you know what skills you have. Most people looking for jobs think that job-content skills are their most important skills. These skills are important, but employers often select job applicants with less experience because of their adaptive or transferable skills.

There are two good reasons for knowing your skills:

1. If you know your skills, you can look for jobs where you are more likely to use those skills. You won't be looking for just "any" job. This increases your chances of finding a job that allows you to be more happy and productive.

2. Employers can't guess what you are good at; you have to tell them. Someone who can give an employer good reasons for hiring them over someone else has a better chance of getting a job offer. For example, a person who convinces an employer that he or she is easy to get along with, willing to work hard, and able to learn quickly may get a job over a person with more experience.

Identifying Your Best Skills

Of the three groups of skills—job content, adaptive, and transferable—which would you guess are the most important to an employer?

This may surprise you, but job content skills are NOT the things an employer stresses the most. You can be an amazing typist, for instance, but if you go to an interview and reveal poor adaptive skills, you probably won't be hired. Being able to use a keyboard does not guarantee success on the job. Developing good self-management and transferable skills make success much more likely.

Take inventory of the skills you already have and the ones you would like to possess by using the following "Skills Checklist." Check the ones that apply to you. Put one check next to each skill that you feel you have and two checks next to each skill you want to use in your next job. For any skill that you'd like to improve, put three checks next to that skill.

Your "Good Worker" Traits

One way to identify important self-management skills is to list the things about yourself that you think make you a good worker.

Complete the exercise that follows to get an idea of some adaptive skills that you already have.

Your Five "Good Worker" Traits List

On the following lines, list five traits you have that make you a good worker. Think about what an employer would like about you.

1. _____

2. _____

3. _____

4. _____

5. _____

Adaptive/Transferable Skills Checklist

Adaptive Skills

_____Accept supervision

_____Get along with people

_____Get things done on time

_____Good attendance

_____Hard worker

_____Honest

_____Punctual

_____Productive

_____Ambitious

_____Capable

_____Cheerful

_____Mature

_____Motivated

_____Conscientious

_____Creative

_____Dependable

_____Efficient

_____Enthusiastic

_____Energetic

_____Flexible

_____Helpful

_____Intuitive

_____Learn quickly

_____Original

_____Persistent

_____Resourceful

_____Take pride in work

_____Solve problems

_____Trustworthy

_____Well organized

Transferable Skills

Working with hardware

_____Assemble things

_____Build things

_____Repair things

_____Drive, operate vehicles

_____Good with hands

_____Use complex equipment

Working with data

_____Analyze

_____Calculate/compute

_____Check for accuracy

_____Classify

_____Compare

_____Count

_____Good with details

_____Keep records

_____Locate information

_____Manage money

_____Record facts/data

_____Take inventory

Working with people

_____Advise

_____Care for people

_____Patient

_____Perceptive

_____Sensitive

_____Diplomatic

_____Good at teaching

_____Good listener

_____Supervise

_____Tactful

_____Sociable

_____Tolerant

Working with words, ideas

_____Verbal communication

_____Original

Adaptive/Transferable Skills Checklist (continued)

Transferable Skills

Working with words, ideas

_____Writing

_____Good memory

_____Create ideas

Leadership

_____Arrange social functions

_____Competitive

_____Decisive

_____Can direct others

_____Can explain things to others

_____Make decisions

_____Work out problems

_____Planning

_____Run meetings

_____Self-confidence

_____Can motivate people

_____Can work out agreements

Creative/Artistic

_____Artistic

_____Drawing

_____Expressive

_____Perform, act

_____Present artistic idea

_____Dance, body movement

Job Content Skills

Job content skills allow you to do a particular job. House painters know how to mix paint and use a brush, among other things. Cashiers in grocery stores use cash registers. A secretary must know how to type.

You have probably gained a number of job content skills already. If you have been active in sports, for example, you know a variety of sports equipment and may be able to work in a sports equipment store. If you know how to cook, that may help you work in a restaurant.

Your Own Job Content Skills List

Make a list of any job content skills you have gained through hobbies, school, sports, working at home, part-time work, volunteer work, or any other activity you can think of. Use the spaces below for your list. Think hard. You have more skills than you think you do!

_____

_____

_____

_____

_____

_____

Now go back and circle the job content skills that you would most like to use in your next job. Later, you can think about various job possibilities that would use these skills.

Your Key Skills List

Look over the skills identification activities you completed in this section, and then answer the following questions:

1. Which three of your adaptive skills do you think are most important for you to emphasize in your job interview?

_____

_____

_____

2. Which three of your transferable skills would you most like to use in your career or next job?

_____

_____

_____

3. Which three of your job-content skills are you most interested in developing or using in a long-term career?

_____

_____

_____

What Is Your Ideal Job?

Writing a Work Statement

You have just gathered quite a bit of information about yourself. You have explored:

- What rewards you want from working
- What job traits you want
- What skills you have and enjoy using

Using this information, see whether you can write a "work statement" for yourself. Your work statement should be a summary of the most important things you have learned about what working means to you. What is the ideal situation for you? You don't have to come up with a specific job for this. Just describe which rewards, job traits, and skills would make you happy in your work.

Read the following sample work statements, written by two students, for some ideas:

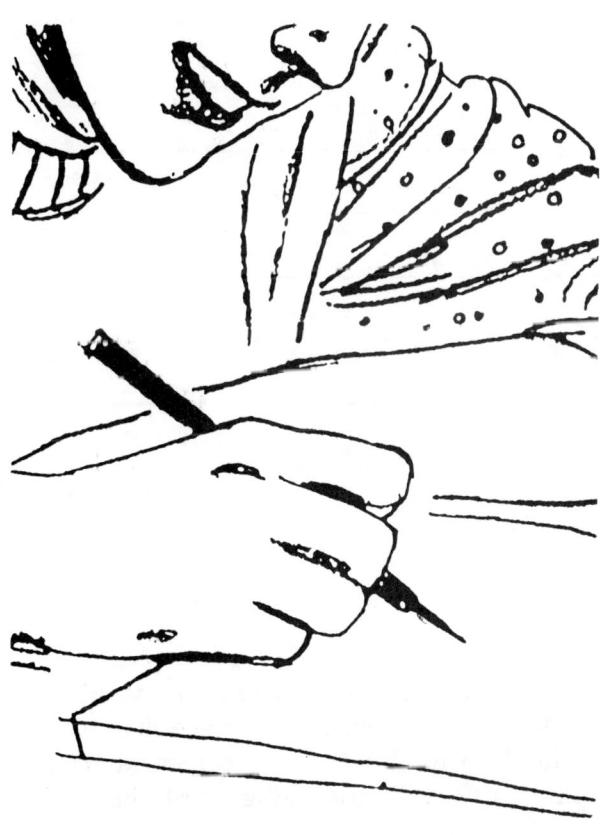

Brian's Work Statement

I will look for a job that will keep me busy throughout the day with a variety of things to do. I'd like to have a lot of contact with people while I'm working. I also like working with numbers and with equipment such as calculators and computers, so my ideal job would involve using those skills. I want to be in a clean, orderly environment (with air conditioning in the summer!) where people look and act like professionals. I don't expect to get rich, but I'd like to earn enough to have some luxuries as well as meet my basic expenses. My ideal job will provide good health insurance and paid vacations, and the chance for promotion if I work hard.

Andrea's Work Statement

I want to work with my hands. I've always liked tinkering with things. I don't want a job where I have to worry about keeping my hands and my clothes clean. In fact, the more casual I can be, the better. I think a small shop of some kind— with a few other people around—would be ideal for me. I like having the responsibility of getting something done myself and figuring out how to do it. My ideal job doesn't have to have great benefits—just a steady paycheck.

Brian and Andrea both have a pretty good idea of what working conditions and benefits they want with their jobs. Now it's your turn. See how much you've learned so far about what kind of career suits you.

My Work Statement

_____

_____

_____

_____

_____

_____

_____

_____

_____

_____

_____

Now that you have some ideas about what kind of work you might like, let's look at ways to gather information for your career interests. But first, answer the following questions for review.

Questions for Review

1. What is the difference between a job and a career?

_____

_____

_____

_____

2. Earning money is one of the rewards of working. What other rewards do you want with your work? (Try to name at least three.)

_____

_____

_____

_____

3. Of the three types of skills (adaptive, transferable, and job content), which is the most important to an employer? Why?

_____

_____

_____

4. Does your work statement give you some ideas of jobs that might suit you? What are they?

_____

_____

_____

_____

_____

_____

_____

_____

Part II

Discovering Jobs and Careers

Researching for Your Future

Have you ever been assigned to do a research paper in school? If so, you may be familiar with the cold chill that runs down your spine at the sound of the word, RESEARCH.

But, reseach can be fun ... especially when the topic is interesting. And what could be more interesting than your own life?

When you do research about jobs that interest you, you are researching your future. Your choice of career could affect where you live, what kind of lifestyle you can afford, what kind of people you know, and much more.

In this section, you'll learn how to get more information on various jobs and careers. You can use this information to help find a job that will satisfy your needs. There are lots of ways to find that information. Let's look at some of the best ones.

The Occupational Outlook Handbook (OOH)

The *Occupational Outlook Handbook,* or *OOH,* is a big book loaded with helpful information. It is published by the U.S. Department of Labor and updated every two years. The *OOH* provides information for about 300 of the most popular jobs in the United States. Over 80 percent of the people in the United States work in one of these jobs, so it is likely that you will find the jobs you are interested in.

When you're exploring job possibilities, the *OOH* is one of the best places to start looking. Each job description is easy to read and includes information on the following:

- The nature of the work
- Future employment outlook
- Earnings
- Related occupations
- Training and education requirements
- Skills required

The following exercises will help you get acquainted with the book. But first, you need to get your hands on the latest edition. Go to your school library or a public library, and ask the librarian to help you find it. You probably won't be allowed to sign the book out, so once you locate a copy, find a comfortable place to sit, and do the exercises that follow.

Getting to Know the OOH

Begin by reading the foreword on one of the first pages of the book. It provides a brief explanation of how this book can be useful to you.

Next, turn to the table of contents. Glance down the columns on these pages to get an idea of how the book is organized.

Checklist of Jobs in the *OOH*

On the next page you will find a checklist derived from a recent *OOH*. Notice that the jobs are arranged within major clusters of related jobs. You can use this list to identify jobs that you may want to learn more about. Look through the entire list and mark each job with one of the following letters:

V Very interested in finding out more about this job.

S Somewhat interested in finding out more about this job.

N Not interested in finding out more about this job.

When you are finished, go back over the checklist again, and underline the five or so jobs that you are particularly interested in.

The OOH Occupations Checklist

**Managerial and Management-
  Related Occupations**
___Accountants and auditors
___Construction and building
  inspectors
___Cost estimators
___Education administrators
___Employment interviewers
___Financial managers
___General managers and top
  executives
___Health services managers
___Hotel managers and assistants
___Inspectors and compliance officers,
  except construction
___Management analysts and
  consultants
___Marketing, advertising, and public
  relations managers
___Personnel, training, and labor
  relations specialists and managers
___Property and real estate managers
___Purchasing agents and managers
___Restaurant and food service
  managers
___Underwriters
___Wholesale and retail buyers

Engineers, Surveyors, and Architects
Engineers
___Aerospace engineers
___Chemical engineers
___Civil engineers
___Electrical and electronics engineers
___Industrial engineers
___Mechanical engineers
___Metallurgical, ceramic, and
  materials engineers
___Mining engineers
___Nuclear engineers
___Petroleum engineers
Architects and surveyors
___Architects
___Landscape architects
___Surveyors

**Natural, Computer, and
  Mathematical Scientists**
*Computer, mathematical, and
  operations research*
___Actuaries
___Computer systems analysts
___Mathematicians
___Operations research analysts
___Statisticians
Life scientists
___Agricultural scientists
___Biological scientists
___Foresters and conservation
  scientists
Physical scientists
___Chemists
___Geologists and geophysicists
___Meteorologists
___Physicists and astronomers

**Lawyers, Social Scientists, Social
  Workers, and Religious Workers**
___Lawyers and judges
Social scientists and urban planners
___Economists
___Psychologists
___Sociologists
___Urban and regional planners
Social and recreation workers
___Human services workers
___Social workers
___Recreation workers
Religious Workers
___Protestant ministers
___Rabbis
___Roman Catholic priests

Teachers, Librarians, and Counselors
___Adult and vocational education
  teachers
___Archivists and curators
___College and university faculty
___Counselors
___Kindergarten and elementary
  school teachers
___Librarians
___Secondary school teachers

**Health Diagnosing and Treating
  Practitioners**
___Chiropractors
___Dentists
___Optometrists

___Physicians
___Podiatrists
___Veterinarians

**Registered Nurses, Pharmacists,
  Dietitians, Therapists and Physician
  Assistants**
___Dietitians and nutritionists
___Occupational therapists
___Pharmacists
___Physical therapists
___Physician assistants
___Recreational therapists
___Registered nurses
___Respiratory therapists
___Speech-language pathologists and
  audiologists

**Health Technologists and
  Technicians**
___Clinical laboratory technologists
  and technicians
___Dental hygienists
___Dispensing opticians
___EEG technologists and technicians
___EKG technicians
___Emergency medical technicians
___Licensed practical nurses
___Medical record technicians
___Nuclear medicine technologists
___Radiologic technologists
___Surgical technicians

Writers, Artists, and Entertainers
Communications
___Public relations specialists
___Radio and television announcers
  and newscasters
___Reporters and correspondents
___Writers and editors
Visual arts
___Designers
___Photographers and camera
  operators
___Visual artists
Performing arts
___Actors, directors, and producers
___Dancers and choreographers
___Musicians

**Technologists and Technicians,
  Except Health**
___Air traffic controllers
___Broadcast technicians

The OOH Occupations Checklist (continued)

___Computer programmers
___Drafters
___Engineering technicians
___Legal assistants
___Library technicians
___Science technicians
___Tool programmers, numerical control

Marketing and Sales Occupations

___Cashiers
___Counter and rental clerks
___Insurance sales workers
___Manufactuers' sales workers
___Real estate agents and brokers
___Retail sales workers
___Securities and financial services sales representatives
___Service sales representatives
___Travel agents
___Wholesale trade sales workers

Administrative Support Occupations, Including Clerical

___Bank tellers
___Bookkeepers and accounting clerks
___Clerical supervisors and managers
___Computer and peripheral equipment operators
___Data entry keyers
___File clerks
___General Office Clerks
___Insurance claims and policy processing occupations
___Postal clerks and mail carriers
___Receptionists and information clerks
___Reservation and transportation ticket agents and travel clerks
___Secretaries
___Statistical clerks
___Stenographers
___Stock clerks
___Teacher aides
___Telephone operators
___Traffic, shipping, and receiving clerks
___Typists and word processors

Service Occupations

___Protective service occupations
___Correction officers
___Firefighting occupations
___Guards
___Police, detectives, and special agents
___Food and beverage preparation and service occupations
___Chefs, cooks, and other kitchen workers
___Food and beverage service occupations
___Health service occupations
___Dental assistants
___Medical assistants
___Nursing aides and psychiatric aides
___Personal service and cleaning occupations
___Barbers
___Childcare workers
___Cosmetologists and related workers
___Flight attendants
___Homemaker-home health aides
___Janitors and cleaners
___Private household workers

Agriculture, Forestry, Fishery, and Related Occupations

___Farm operators and managers
___Fishers, hunters, and trappers
___Timber cutting and logging workers

Mechanics, Installers, and Repairers

___Aircraft mechanics and engine specialists
___Automotive body repairers
___Automotive mechanics
___Commerical and industrial electronic equipment repairers
___Communications equipment mechanics
___Computer service technicians
___Diesel mechanics
___Electronic home entertainment equipment repairers
___Elevator installers and repairers

___Farm equipment mechanics
___General maintenance mechanics
___Heating, air-conditioning, and refrigeration mechanics
___Home applicance and power tool repairers
___Industrial machinery repairers
___Line installers and cable splicers
___Millwrights
___Mobile heavy equipment mechanics
___Motorcycle, boat, and small-engine mechanics
___Musical instrument repairers and tuners
___Office machine and cash register servicers
___Telephone installers and repairers
___Vending machine servicers and repairers

Construction Trades and Extractive Occupations

___Bricklayers and stonemasons
___Carpenters
___Carpet installers
___Concrete masons and terrazzo workers
___Drywall workers and lathers
___Electricians
___Glaziers
___Insulation workers
___Painters and paperhangers
___Plasterers
___Plumbers and pipefitters
___Roofers
___Roustabouts
___Sheet-metal workers
___Structural and reinforcing metal workers
___Tilesetters

Production Occupations

___Apparel workers
___Bindery workers
___Blue-collar worker supervisors
___Boilermakers
___Butchers and meatcutters
___Compositors and typesetters
___Dental laboratory technicians

The OOH Occupations Checklist (continued)

___Electric power generating plant operators and power distributors and dispatchers
___Inspectors, testers, and graders
___Jewelers
___Lithographic and photoengraving workers
___Machinists
___Metalworking and plastic-working machine operators
___Numerical-control machine-tool operators
___Ophthalmic laboratory technicians
___Painting and coating machine operators

___Photographic process workers
___Precision assemblers
___Printing press operators
___Shoe and leather workers and repairers
___Stationary engineers
___Textile machinery operators
___Tool-and-die makers
___Upholsterers
___Water and wastewater treatment plant operators
___Welders, cutters, and welding machine operators
___Woodworkers

Transportation and Material Moving Occupations
___Aircraft pilots
___Busdrivers
___Material moving equipment operators
___Truckdrivers
Handlers, Equipment Cleaners, Helpers, and Laborers
___Construction trades helpers
Job Opportunities in the Armed Forces
___Military

Selecting *OOH* Jobs for More Exploration

Look over the previous activity, and select the five jobs from the list that you are most interested in learning more about. List those jobs here:

1. _____

2. _____

3. _____

4. _____

5. _____

Use a copy of a current *OOH* to look up the jobs you have listed. The table of contents lists the various jobs and the page numbers where they can be found. Different editions may use different jobs titles for similar jobs, so if you can't find the jobs you listed above in your *OOH*, find ones with similar titles.

You may also find it helpful to read the section in the *OOH* titled "How To Get the Most from the Handbook" before reading the actual job descriptions.

When you are done, complete the following worksheet for the top three jobs on your list. Use additional blank pieces of paper as needed for additional jobs.

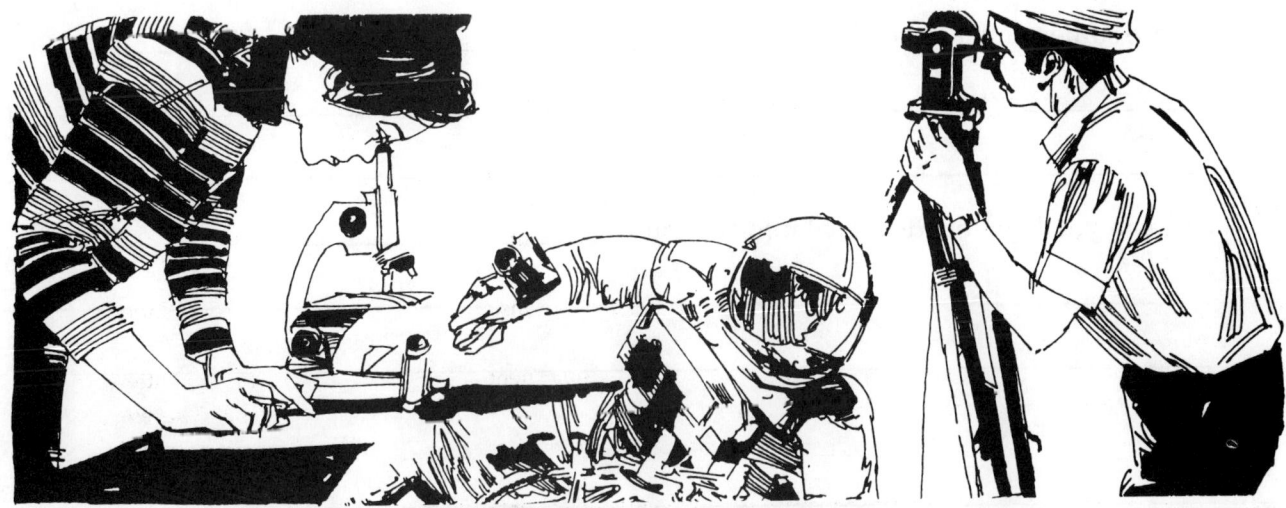

OOH Job Description Worksheet

Job Title:_____OOH Edition: _____

1. What is the nature of the work? _____

_____

_____

2. What are the working conditions of this job? _____

_____

_____

3. What did you find out about employment trends for this job? _____

_____

_____

4. What are the qualifications and training requirements for this job? _____

_____

_____

5. What is the job outlook for this job? _____

_____

_____

6. What are the expected earnings of this job? _____

7. What are some related occupations? _____

_____

_____

8. Where can you look for additional information? _____

_____

_____

OOH Job Description Worksheet

Job Title:_____OOH Edition: _____

1. What is the nature of the work? _____

   _____

   _____

2. What are the working conditions of this job?_____

   _____

   _____

3. What did you find out about employment trends for this job?

   _____

   _____

4. What are the qualifications and training requirements for this job? _____

   _____

   _____

5. What is the job outlook for this job?_____

   _____

   _____

6. What are the expected earnings of this job? _____

7. What are some related occupations? _____

   _____

   _____

8. Where can you look for additional information? _____

   _____

   _____

OOH Job Description Worksheet

Job Title:_____OOH Edition: _____

1. What is the nature of the work? _____

    _____

    _____

2. What are the working conditions of this job?_____

    _____

    _____

3. What did you find out about employment trends for this job?_____

    _____

    _____

4. What are the qualifications and training requirements for this job? _____

    _____

    _____

5. What is the job outlook for this job? _____

    _____

    _____

6. What are the expected earnings of this job?_____

7. What are some related occupations? _____

    _____

    _____

8. Where can you look for additional information? _____

    _____

    _____

What Did You Find Out?

Now that you know more about these jobs than you did before, do they still interest you? If so, go on to the next group of exercises for researching jobs. If not, go back to your list of job possibilities, and pick another job to check out in the *OOH*.

Use a blank sheet of paper for each possibility you research, and use the questions from the "*OOH* Job Description Worksheet" to gather information. Keep doing this until you find a job that you really want to know more about.

Talking to People Who Know about the Job

The *Occupational Outlook Handbook* can tell you a lot about a job, but it can't tell you everything. After you've learned all you can about a job from the OOH, it's time to find someone who does the work you think you might like to do.

How do you find someone to talk to? Here are some ways:

- Ask your school guidance counselor for suggestions.
- Ask your parents, your friends' parents, other relatives, neighbors, teachers, or anyone else who might know someone.
- Use the Yellow Pages of your telephone book to locate someone in your field of interest. If necessary, ask someone for help with this.

How to Interview People about the Work They Do

If you're shy, this part of your research may give you butterflies in your stomach. It involves talking to people who know more about the job you are interested in and asking them about it. We call this an information interview.

Most people truly enjoy talking about their work. They may even be flattered that you want to talk to them. You can do your entire interview over the telephone or meet with the person face to face. That will depend on what is convenient for them and what you prefer.

When you find a person to talk to about a job, make a telephone call to explain that you are researching jobs. Say that you are interested in learning more about the work that person does. Ask for a convenient meeting place and time.

If the person tells you to call back at a certain time, be sure to do that. Don't call at 3:15 p.m. if the instructions were to call at 3:00 p.m.

Use the following worksheet for help in asking questions during your interview. Ask other questions that you can think of as well. Remember, you're talking to someone who does what you might do someday!

Wait until after the interview to fill in the answers. You can jot down notes if you want, but it's important to listen carefully during the conversation. Then you can write brief descriptions of what you learned. When you have finished with your interview, remember to thank the person for taking the time to talk with you. (He or she could turn out to be a job contact some day!)

Information Interview Worksheet

Person Interviewed:_____Date of Interview:_____

Person's Organization: _____Title: _____

Phone Number:_____

Organization's Address: _____

  1. Do you like your work? _____Why? _____

    _____

    _____

  2. What do you do most of the time? _____

    _____

    _____

    _____

  3. What are the responsibilities of your job? _____

    _____

    _____

    _____

  4. What are your biggest satisfactions on the job? _____

    _____

    _____

  5. What are the biggest headaches or drawbacks that you've found with your job? _____

    _____

    _____

  6. How did you get your job? _____

    _____

    _____

Information Interview Worksheet (continued)

7. What kind of training did you get, and where did you receive it?

_____

_____

_____

8. What skills does your work require?

_____

_____

_____

9. What advice could you offer to a person entering your field?

_____

_____

_____

10. Write down anything else you learned in the information interview that wasn't covered by the questions above.

_____

_____

_____

_____

_____

_____

_____

_____

_____

_____

Information Interview Worksheet

Person Interviewed:_____Date of Interview:_____

Person's Organization: _____Title: _____

Phone Number:_____

Organization's Address: _____

1. Do you like your work? _____Why?_____

   _____

   _____

2. What do you do most of the time? _____

   _____

   _____

   _____

3. What are the responsibilities of your job? _____

   _____

   _____

   _____

4. What are your biggest satisfactions on the job? _____

   _____

   _____

5. What are the biggest headaches or drawbacks that you've found with your job? _____

   _____

   _____

6. How did you get your job? _____

   _____

   _____

Information Interview Worksheet (continued)

7. What kind of training did you get, and where did you receive it?

_____

_____

_____

8. What skills does your work require?

_____

_____

_____

9. What advice could you offer to a person entering your field?

_____

_____

_____

10. Write down anything else you learned in the information interview that wasn't covered by the questions above.

_____

_____

_____

_____

_____

_____

_____

_____

_____

Information Interview Summary Worksheet

After you have completed one or more of the "Interview Information Worksheets," answer the questions that follow.

Person Interviewed: _____ Occupation: _____

1. Is this still a job you think you'd like?_____Why?_____

   _____

   _____

2. What training, experience, or skills do you need to qualify for this job?_____

   _____

   _____

   Can you acquire those things?_____

3. Were you surprised by anything the person you interviewed told you?_____

   _____

   _____

4. Do you think it would be helpful to talk to more people in this field? Why?_____

   _____

   _____

5. Are there other related jobs that might be closer to what you are looking for?_____

   _____

   What are they? _____

   _____

6. What are some related occupations? _____

   _____

   _____

7. Where can you look for additional information?_____

   _____

Information Interview Summary Worksheet

After you have completed one or more of the "Interview Information" Worksheets, answer the questions that follow.

Person Interviewed: _____ Occupation: _____

1. Is this still a job you think you'd like? _____ Why? _____

   _____

   _____

2. What training, experience, or skills do you need to qualify for this job? _____

   _____

   _____

   Can you acquire those things? _____

3. Were you surprised by anything the person you interviewed told you? _____

   _____

   _____

4. Do you think it would be helpful to talk to more people in this field? Why? _____

   _____

   _____

5. Are there other related jobs that might be closer to what you are looking for? _____ _____

   What are they? _____

   _____

6. What are some related occupations? _____

   _____

   _____

7. Where can you look for additional information? _____

   _____

   _____

Other Ways To Find Out about Jobs

Volunteer Work

Doing volunteer work is an excellent way to gain skills needed for paid jobs in a similar occupation. It also gives you an inside look at a field you might pursue as a career some day.

Volunteering can help you see whether things such as working conditions, training, and the skills required by the job, match what you are looking for in your work. Volunteering can also open the door to a future job.

You won't have to look far for volunteer opportunities. Many communities have a community services publication listing nonprofit organizations that use volunteers. Look in your local newspaper for notices. Check bulletin boards at libraries, schools, churches, and grocery stores. Your parents, school counselor, librarian, or others can help you find information about volunteer possibilities.

Let's try an exercise to help you see what kinds of volunteer activities might interest you. Fill out the "Volunteer Interest Worksheet" that follows.

Locate a source of information about volunteer opportunities in your community. Ask parents, teachers, or school guidance counselors for help with this if you need it. Find two volunteer possibilities that spark your interest. Then use the following worksheets as a guide to looking into these possibilities.

Volunteer Interest Worksheet #1

Name of Organization: _____

Person You Spoke With: _____ Title: _____

Phone number: _____ Date: _____

1. What kind of organization is it? (social service agency, school, church, etc.) _____
_____

2. What types of services does this organization provide to the community?
_____
_____

3. What interested you about this particular type of organization? _____
_____
_____

4. What skills would you be using if you worked for this organization?_____
_____
_____

5. What skills would this work help you develop? (Remember to think about adaptive and transferable skills, not just job content skills.)
_____
_____

6. When can you work for this organization? Be specific about days and hours you can work.
_____
_____

7. Is there a possibility that your volunteer work for this organization could eventually lead to paid work on a part-time basis?
_____
_____

Volunteer Interest Worksheet #2

Name of Organization: _____

Person You Spoke With: _____ Title: _____

Phone number: _____ Date: _____

1. What kind of organization is it? (social service agency, school, church, etc.) _____
   _____

2. What types of services does this organization provide to the community?_____
   _____
   _____

3. What interested you about this particular type of organization? _____
   _____
   _____

4. What skills would you be using if you worked for this organization?_____
   _____
   _____

5. What skills would this work help you develop? (Remember to think about adaptive and transferable skills, not just job content skills.)
   _____
   _____

6. When can you work for this organization? Be specific about days and hours you can work. _____
   _____
   _____

7. Is there a possibility that your volunteer work for this organization could eventually lead to paid work on a part-time basis?
   _____
   _____

Evaluating the Information You Gathered on Volunteering

Now it's time to make some choices about the information you've gathered. Answer the following questions:

1. Do you think that volunteer work is something you want to do, either now or in the future? Why or why not?

_____

_____

_____

_____

2. Do either of the two volunteer possibilities you just researched still interest you, or do you want to look into other possibilities? Please explain.

_____

_____

_____

_____

Use the checklist that follows to help you decide which of your options is the best one. Put a check mark in each column when your answer is "Yes."

By looking at the number of check marks you put in each column, you can determine which volunteer possibility makes the most sense for you.

Remember that even though this is unpaid work, you are expected to show up for work when you say you will or give notice when you will be absent. It is also important that you know, before you make a commitment, how you will get to and from work.

Volunteer Options Checklist

Volunteer Interest Worksheet #1

_____I like the purpose of this organization.

_____The work I would be doing would use some of my best skills.

_____I think I would enjoy the work I would be doing.

_____This organization would help me develop valuable skills for the future.

_____My schedule allows me to work the days and number of hours this organization prefers.

_____I am able to get to and from the work site reliably.

Volunteer Intererst Worksheet #2

_____I like the purpose of this organization.

_____The work I would be doing would use some of my best skills.

_____I think I would enjoy the work I would be doing.

_____This organization would help me develop valuable skills for the future.

_____My schedule allows me to work the days and number of hours this organization prefers.

_____I am able to get to and from the work site reliably.

Part-Time and Summer Employment

Have you ever had a part-time job? Have you ever thought about getting a part-time job? Many students think of part-time employment only as a way to make money. By thinking of it that way, they often take the first thing that comes along.

But you don't have to wait until you are sure of your career path to look for work with the rewards you explored in the first section of this book. There may be part-time work available to you now, or over the next several years, that can help you start developing your career path—as well as provide a means for earning money.

The next section of this book will help you figure out what sort of part-time or summer job will make the most sense for you.

Questions for Review

1. What are some resources you can use to find information about jobs?

_____

_____

_____

_____

_____

2. How did the information you got from the *Occupational Outlook Handbook* affect your opinion of jobs that interested you?

_____

_____

_____

_____

_____

3. What are some of the things you can learn from an information interview?

_____

_____

_____

_____

_____

4. What are some ways that volunteer or part-time work can help you on your career path?

_____

_____

_____

_____

Part III

Planning For Jobs and Careers

Plan for Success

You have now learned quite a bit about your skills, various job titles and what they require. Short term, you may decide to get or keep a part-time job. Long term, you may have some ideas about what career you want to consider.

In either case, planning now will help you get a better job now or a more satisfying career and lifestyle later. This section of the book will help you begin your planning.

In the following story, read how one person figured out how to look for a particular kind of job rather than just "any" job. If you use your imagination, you can figure out how to find a job that is interesting to you!

Veronica Figures Out What Type of Job She Wants

Veronica dropped her school books on the kitchen table and sat down with her chin in her hands. She felt discouraged. She wanted an after-school job, but she had already tried two different jobs, and neither one of them had worked out. Scooping ice cream in an ice cream shop had been fun for the first couple of weeks, but then the charm wore off. There was no challenge.

Selling candy door-to-door in the neighborhood was even worse. She felt like she just wasn't getting anywhere.

Now here she sat, doing nothing, which was worse yet! Her dog, Pepper, came over and put her head on Veronica's knee, as if to sympathize. Pepper was a great dog. Veronica scratched the dog's ear, lost in thought, when suddenly she had an idea. She remembered how much she had enjoyed training Pepper when the dog had first come to live at their house.

Pepper had been kind of wild then, and no one except Veronica was successful with her training. Veronica had felt a lot of pride in that. "You're a natural!" her mother said. "You and animals just seem to understand each other."

Now it occurred to Veronica that a job working with animals would be a great job for her. She pulled out a notebook and a pencil and began making a list of all the possibilities.

- Dog trainer
- Veterinarian
- Dog Groomer
- Horse Stable
- Humane Society
- Zoo
- Petshop

Veronica was excited. Suddenly, there were so many possibilities! If she asked around some and did some research, she knew she could come up with even more ideas.

Veronica Considers Her Options

Veronica did ask around, and she did some research. She made telephone calls to various employers, looked into volunteer possibilities, and talked to friends, neighbors—anyone who might have some ideas for her. She even thought about starting her own small business of taking care of pets while their owners were out of town. Finally, she narrowed her possibilities down to the three best options. Then she asked for interviews with employers.

Veronica's First Interview

Of the three interviews Veronica tried to arrange, two were scheduled. The third one wasn't hiring at the time. The day of the first interview, Veronica's mother dropped her off at the veterinarian's office where Veronica was hoping to work.

As soon as she walked in the office, Veronica knew something was wrong. There were two other people applying for jobs there, a boy and a girl. They were dressed differently from Veronica. They wore dress slacks, and the boy even wore a tie. Veronica had on blue jeans. She wished she had given more thought to what she should wear.

"Fill this out," the receptionist told Veronica, handing her a piece of paper. It was an application form. Veronica's heart sank as she read it. She didn't know what answers to put down for at least half the questions!

Soon she was ushered into a small room to talk with a woman named Doctor Bianco, who seemed very busy. The doctor asked questions quickly. Veronica's conversation with her went like this:

Dr. Bianco:	What hours can you work, Miss Smith?
Veronica:	Um, well, whenever you need me, I guess. After school, that is. (Suddenly, she remembered band practice on Tuesdays and Thursdays. Should she tell her about that?)
Dr. Bianco:	How will you get to work?
Veronica:	Well, um, actually, I haven't thought about that yet. I figured I'd work that out once I got the job.
Dr. Bianco:	(frowning) Why do you want to work here, Miss Smith?
Veronica:	I really love animals. I think it would be neat to work around animals.
Dr. Bianco:	(still frowning) What makes you qualified for this job?
Veronica:	I guess I thought I'd be pretty good with the animals.
Dr. Bianco:	Well, thank you for coming in. We'll let you know in a few days.

Veronica left in a hurry. In fact, she had never been so glad to get out of a place in her life.

What Did Veronica Do Wrong?

Being unprepared for an interview is an unpleasant experience. Can you think of three things that went wrong for Veronica? List them in the following spaces.

1. _____

_____

2. _____

_____

3. _____

_____

Now read about how things went for Veronica the next time she interviewed for a job.

Veronica's Second Interview

Veronica's next interview was at a pet shop. She arrived at the shop wearing one of her best school outfits, clean and pressed. When she sat down to fill out the application form, she pulled out a notebook in which she had written down this information:

- Names, addresses, and telephone numbers of former employers
- Names, addresses, and telephone numbers of three references (people who knew she was reliable and hard working)
- Names and addresses of schools she had attended

Veronica handed back the application with all the information filled in. Then she was ushered into a small room for a conversation with the owner of the pet shop, Mr. Collie O'Brien.

Mr. O'Brien: What hours are you available for work, Miss Smith?

Veronica: I can work from three o'clock until nine o'clock on Monday, Wednesday, and Friday, and any hours you might need me for on Saturday.

Mr. O'Brien: How will you get to work?

Veronica: There is a bus that runs every 20 minutes from both my school and my house. My mother is available to drive me on Saturdays.

Mr. O'Brien: Why do you want to work here?

Veronica: I love working with animals, and I also enjoy contact with people. I would be able to give customers a lot of tips on how to care for and train their new pets. I think that would be good for business, and that would give me a lot of satisfaction.

Mr. O'Brien: What makes you qualified for this job?

Veronica: The qualifications I have now are experience with animals and an ability to talk with people. I'm a responsible person, and I learn new things quickly.

Mr. O'Brien: (smiling) How soon can you start?

What Did Veronica Do Right?

This time, Veronica was prepared for the interview. Can you think of three things she did differently from the first one? List them below.

1. _____

_____

2. _____

_____

3. _____

_____

Tips for a Successful Interview

Not every employer will ask the exact same questions. Also, being well prepared for an interview won't guarantee that you'll get the job. But if you are prepared, your chances are a lot better! Here are some tips you can use when the time comes for your first interview:

■ Dress appropriately: not too dressy and not too casual. A safe way to dress is to dress like your supervisor is likely to be dressed.

■ Be well groomed.

■ Carry the information you'll need to fill out an application.

■ Be ready to talk with confidence about your skills, knowledge, and experience.

■ Have a clear idea of when you can work and how you will get there.

■ Be at the interview a few minutes early.

Now read on for some ideas on how to begin laying a foundation for your career.

Begin Making Career Plans Now

Do you know what the figure of speech, "setting something in concrete," means? It means that once something is done, it can't be undone. For example, a decision that is "set in concrete" cannot be changed.

But career planning is not like this. Whatever you decide now can be changed later on as you learn more about yourself and what you want. Most people your age will change their career plans several times. You are not expected to make major career decisions at this time in your life, if you're not ready.

Rather, this book is meant to help you develop the skills to make good career plans as you need to. The decisions you make now do not have to be "set in concrete."

The topics we have covered in this book include:

- Knowing the difference between jobs and careers
- Discovering job traits, rewards, and skills that interest you
- Learning to use the Occupational Outlook Handbook
- Researching volunteer and part-time employment opportunities

What are some other ways that you can plan now to start laying a solid foundation for your career? List as many things you can do now in the space provided below.

_____
_____
_____
_____
_____
_____
_____
_____
_____
_____
_____
_____
_____
_____
_____
_____
_____
_____
_____

Did your list include any of the following?

- Work for good grades in school
- Develop hobbies that you enjoy
- Continue to strengthen your best skills
- Save money for future education or training
- Take classes that apply to your career
- Participate in activities that relate to your career interests

Planning for the Future

For your final exercise, see if you can make a plan for the career path you seem most interested in right now. Remember, this is not set in concrete! In the years ahead, your interests may change, you might develop different skills, and new opportunities might arise. But for now, make a plan based on what you know about yourself at this point in time.

Career Planning Worksheet

Review any section of this book as needed to help answer these questions.

1. The career that interests me now is:

   _____

   _____

2. The key skills that I have and would most like to use in my career include:

   _____

   _____

   _____

   _____

3. The classes I need to take during high school for this career path include:

   _____

   _____

   _____

   _____

4. School-related activities I will use to help me on my career path are:

   _____

   _____

   _____

   _____

5. Activities outside of school (volunteer work, part-time work, etc.) that make sense for me are:

   _____

   _____

   _____

   _____

Career Planning Worksheet (continued)

6. Education or training after high school that I need to qualify for this career includes:

_____

_____

_____

7. My goals (personal or other) for the next year include:

_____

_____

_____

For the next three years:

_____

_____

_____

For the next five years:

_____

_____

_____

8. Any other comments:

_____

_____

_____

_____

_____

_____

Questions for Review

1. How did Veronica go about fining a better job, and what does this mean to you?

_____

_____

_____

_____

_____

_____

2. What are the most important ways to prepare for a job interview?

_____

_____

_____

_____

_____

_____

3. Can you think of some reasons why it is wise to begin making career plans now, even if you change your mind?

_____

_____

_____

_____

_____

_____

_____